The Business Plan and *Beyond!*

Beginners Guide Book

RG Bud Phelps

ISBN-13: 978-1481883733
ISBN-10: 1481883739

Contents

Acknowledgements

I would like to take this opportunity to acknowledge the contributors to various chapters in this book: Stu Spero, Professor at Nebraska Wesleyan University; Darrell K. Stock, Attorney at Law; Jim Mastera, retired Banker; Ed Nix, Leadership Coach/Trainer; Rich Oehlerking, retired Insurance Agent; and The Heritage Foundation a research and educational institution—a think tank—whose mission is to formulate and promote conservative public policies based on the principles of free enterprise, limited government, individual freedom, traditional American values, and a strong national defense. In addition; I thank my daughter Bridget for her editing assistance, my son-in-law Don for his assistance in seeking out graphics for the cover, and my daughter Shauna for applying her graphic skills in producing the cover.

Disclaimer

The information supplied herein is general in nature and intended for informational purposes only. It is not to be construed in any way as tax or legal advice. You should consult with a trained professional familiar with the laws and regulations of your area for specific advice regarding any of the information supplied in the chapters of this book.

Introduction

"The Business Plan and *Beyond*" – Beginner's Guide Book, is a reference book for individuals wanting to start their own business. This "Beginner's Guide Book" is a tool that will help individuals going through the preparatory stages of planning a new business. Too many people are so anxious to sell their new widgets or provide their new services that they don't stop long enough to lay out the important factors for their new business.

This *is* my second book about the owner/managers' role in business. My first book is titled, "Cover Your Nut" - Practical Accounting in Plain English for the Real World, was my introduction to practical accounting. This is an extension of the accounting and management needs that are so necessary plus input from key professional team's experiences in the needs of small businesses.

My 50 years working in a variety of businesses has given me the experiences and knowledge to bring you this valuable reference book. This "Beginner's Guide Book" is a tool that will help you in the development of your new business.

Owners and managers need the ability to read and understand their Financial Statements to properly manage their small business through each business cycle. It also gives them the skills to present these statements to their lenders. The owners/managers must control their business problems, and not let these problems control them.

The businessman that takes the time to go through the steps laid out in this book to properly develop their new business has a much better opportunity to be successful. Time spent at the beginning will pay dividends throughout the life of the business.

Remember, the major reason anyone starts a business should be "to make money," it isn't just a fun hobby. The small business manager must understand how to provide themselves with reports that will monitor the operation of their businesses monthly, quarterly, and annually. The development of a Chart of Accounts, Understanding Financial Statements, Management Footprints/Ratios, and Internal Controls will be covered in the "General Accounting Chapter."

The Business Plan and Beyond is meant to be a guide book to give you help, when and where help is most needed. All individuals starting out in business will benefit from a guide book that provides them information for the development and monitoring of their businesses, and controls to safeguard their company when challenges occur.

On page 4 under the heading Acknowledgments, I have introduced you to my team of experts that are sharing their knowledge of key support functions, giving you the inside track for the development of "The Business Plan and *Beyond!*"

The Business Development chapter covers (a workable outline) of a Business Plan, and the Professional Support Team.

The General Accounting chapter will cover the Chart of Accounts, Financial Statements, useful Management Footprints, Financial Statement Ratios, and Internal Controls (to safeguard what goes on in your business).

Stu Spero, Professor at Nebraska Wesleyan University contributed to the development of **"The Business Plan"** section.

Darrell K. Stock, Attorney at Law, covers **"Legal Needs of Small Businesses."**

Jim Mastera retired Banker, covers **"Financing Your Small Business."**

Rich Oehlerking retired Insurance Agent, covers **"Insurance Needs of Small Businesses."**

"Government Information Relative to Small Businesses," What Government is? The Structure of Taxes, Checklist for Starting a Business, and Excess Government Regulations (Includes "The Heritage Foundation" article-"The 10 Worst Regulations of 2012")

Ed Nix, Leadership Coach / Trainer, covers **"Leadership."**

Reading and including this book in your business library doesn't guarantee success but not doing some of the things suggested could guarantee failure.

The "Business Plan and Beyond" – Beginner's Guide Book, is a key start-up reference guide book that could put you in the company of the small percentage of start-up businesses that are successful.

Chapter One
Business Development

Business Development comprises of a number of tasks and processes, generally aiming at developing and implementing growth opportunities.

The key sections for this chapter are:

- **The Business Plan**

    Stu Spero, a professor of Business Administration at Nebraska Wesleyan University for over 20 years, contributed to the development of this "Business Plan" section by both critiquing and adding important key items throughout. Stu is a former Director of the Lincoln, Nebraska office of the Nebraska Business Development Center. He holds masters degrees from Ball State University and University of Nebraska-Lincoln. He is also a former small business owner, and as a member of SCORE, he has been a valued presenter of the business plan section of their workshops for over 25 years.

- **Professional Support Team**

The Business Plan

The act of planning your "Business Plan" helps individuals think things through thoroughly, to study and research the facts relative to starting your new business, and to look at all your ideas **critically** and **honestly**. The "Business Plan" is not just a document you have been told is necessary to develop, but a study proving to individuals and others that their business is feasible.

The "Business Plan" format presented herein is a general and practical outline to give you a guide in the development of your personal business plan. Remember, first the individuals are preparing the Business Plan for themselves; therefore the plan should be modified to fit your personal small businesses needs. The suggested outline is presented in this manner to cover items necessary in most businesses; some may not be pertinent to your business. Don't feel every item mentioned must be covered. Discard the ones which are not needed, and as stated earlier, modify the plan to fit your business.

The Business Plan takes time. Be prepared to spend an adequate amount of time to properly develop your personal business plan, don't rush it. If prepared properly; costly, perhaps disastrous, mistakes can be avoided. A **Practical Approach** to your "Business Plan" must be developed around guidelines covering everything needed to present this plan for yourself, investors, and/or lenders.

A template of a business plan will be available on my website, as well as supportive Financial Statement templates, such as the ones you will need to include in the Financial Section. The templates can be downloaded with this link, http://www.budspracticalaccounting.com.

The following "Business Plan Outline" is presented with details of each section to follow:

"Business Plan Outline"

- **Executive Summary**

- **General Company Description**

- **Marketing Plan**

- **Operational Plan**

- **Management and Organizations**

- **Financial Section**

Executive Summary

The "Executive Summary" should be written last, as it is a summary outline of the business plan. Not all business plans will require an executive summary; if your plan is fewer than 10 to 20 pages it may not be necessary to include one.

The purpose of the Executive Summary is to give the reader the essence of the Business Plan in a short narrative in such a way as to develop interest to continue reading the entire plan. Include everything you would cover in a short interview; keeping it to two pages or less. The suggested length of each section may run from one to four sentences dependent upon the need for detailed explanations.

The Financial Plan section may need to be more detailed, especially if applying for a loan or seeking funding from other sources. If that is the case state clearly the amount you require for the business as your lender or investor will be reading this section first. After listing the amount, show precisely how you are going to use it, and how the money will make your business more profitable, thereby ensuring repayment of the loan.

The goal will be to highlight the essential information in your Business Plan with the Executive Summary causing the reader to want to finish going through the entire plan. One to two paragraphs maximum on each section with a two page maximum for your Executive Summary.

Executive Summary Outline

- **General Company Description**

- **Products and/or Services**

- **Marketing Plan**

- **Operational Plan**

- **Management and Organization**

- **Financial Plan**

.

Review of Goals for your Executive Summary

Make it Enthusiastic and Realistic

Make it Professional

Make it Complete

Make it Concise

One to two paragraphs maximum on each item

One to two pages maximum for the Executive Summary

"The Business Plan Outline"

General Company Description
Products and/or Services
Marketing Plan
Operational Plan
Management and Organization
Financial Plan with Projections
Startup Expenses and Capitalization

General Company Description

What business will you be in?

What will you sell or have as a service?

Mission Statement

Many companies have a brief mission statement, usually in 30 words or fewer, explaining their reason for being and their guiding principles. If you want to draft a mission statement, this would be a good place to put it in the plan.

Example:

Bristol-Myers Squibb- to discover, develop and deliver innovative medicines that help patients prevail over serious diseases.

14

Company Goals and Objectives

Company Goals (broad and general)

What destination do you want your business to reach? A goal might be to have a healthy, successful company that is a leader in customer service and that has a loyal customer following.

Objectives (specific)

Objectives are progress markers along the way to goal achievement. Objectives might be annual sales targets and some specific measures of customer satisfaction.

Business Philosophy

What is important to you in your business?

Market

State briefly what the market will be for your business. You will need a more thorough explanation in the **Marketing Plan** section.

Industry

Briefly describe your industry here. (Manufacturing, Food service) Is it a growth industry? (New/Old) What changes do you foresee in the industry, short term and long term? How will your company be poised to take advantage of these changes?

Describe your most important company strengths

What factors will make your company succeed?

What background experience, skills, and strengths do you personally bring to this new venture?

Legal Structure of ownership:

Sole Proprietor, Partnership, Corporation, Limited Liability Corporation (LLC)

Give the reason why you selected this structure.

Products and/or Services

Describe in depth your products or services

Insert pictures or descriptive examples where appropriate. (It may be best to insert detailed descriptions here and photos in your **Appendices**)

What factors will give your business a competitive advantage?

Include level of quality or unique proprietary features.

What are the pricing, service fees, or specialty features about your products or services?

Marketing Plan

Why you should include Market Research?

Marketing begins with careful, systematic, research. You should not assume that you already know about your intended market; research may be needed to make sure you're business is on track. Use planning process as your opportunity to uncover data and to question your marketing efforts.

How is Market Research done and what types are they?

There are two kinds of Market Research: Primary and Secondary.

Primary Market Research

Primary Market Research is gathering data relative to your specific business; whether this is hired, or done by yourself. Examples: Do your own traffic count at a proposed location; use the yellow pages to identify competitors; do surveys or focus-group interviews to learn about local consumer preferences. This do-it-yourself approach can be very effective and save you money.

Secondary Market Research

Secondary Market Research is utilizing published information such as industry profiles, trade journals, newspapers, magazines, census data, and demographic profiles.

In your Marketing Plan – be as specific as possible

The Marketing plan will be the basis of all important sales projections therefore you should be as specific as possible, giving statistics, numbers, and the sources of your information.

Facts about your industry

- What is the total size of the market?
- What is your business's percentage share of the market?
- Growth trends in your target market?
- What barriers does your business face, and how will you overcome them? Such as: changes in technology, regulations, the economy, or the industry

Features and Benefits about your Product or Service

- Describe the most important Features about your products and why (explain).
- Describe the most important Benefits about your products and Why (explain).
- What after-sale services are included (explain).

Customers

- Identify your targeted customers (their characteristics and their geographic locations).
- Identify your most important customer group (age, gender, location, income level, social class and occupation, education, and specialty).

- For business customers, the demographic factors might be: (industry, location, size, technology, quality, and price preferences).

Competition

- What products or services will compete with you? (How will your products or services compare with them?)
- What are their strengths and weaknesses?
- List your major competitors (Names & Addresses)
- Will they compete with you across the board?
- In a few words explain your business's pluses compared to your competition.

Niche

In one short paragraph, define your business's products or services niche (your unique corner of the market).

Promotion

How will you get the word out to your customers?

Advertising

- What media, why, and how often?
- Identify low-cost methods for your promotions
- Will you use methods other than paid advertising (trade shows, catalogs, dealer incentives, word of mouth, or special networks)

- What plans are needed for graphic image support (logo design, business cards, letterheads, brochures, signage, and interior design)?
- Will your business have a system to identify repeat customers?

Promotional Budget

- How much do you plan on spending for your promotional items shown above?
- Amount of Promotional budget shown in start-up costs.
- Promotional budget for ongoing promotion.
- Specific proposed promotional activities (grand opening and first year; sales & events).

Pricing

- Explain your methods of setting prices (such as: average prices, competing on quality and service).
- Do pricing strategies fit with your competitive analysis?
- How important is price as a competitive factor?
- What are your customer service & credit policies?

Proposed Location

- What does your business want and need in a location?
- How important is your business location to your customers?
- Where is your competition located? (Is there an advantage to locate close to your competition?)

Operational Plan

Write an explanation of the daily operation of your business, its location, equipment, people needs, processes, and surrounding environment.

Production

- How and where are your business's products or services produced?
- Explain your business's methods of (production techniques, quality control, customer service, inventory control, and Product or Service development).

Location

- What is your business's location needs (amount of space, type of building, zoning, power and utilities)?
- Is Access an important factor to your location (walk-in access, parking needs and requirements, access to transportation)?

Build/Buy or Lease your business space

- Develop cost estimates covering your occupation expenses (rent, maintenance, utilities, insurance, initial remodeling costs, or initial construction).
- Who will pay for remodeling/renovation?
- Consult with your attorney regarding any contractual obligations.

Legal Requirements

- Describe the following: (licensing, permits, environmental and industry regulations, zoning).

Personnel

- Number of employees (full and part time).
- Type of need (skilled, unskilled, professional).
- Where and how the right employees will be found.
- Quality of existing staff (if buying a business).
- Pay structure.
- Training methods and requirements.
- Assignment of tasks (who does what).
- Develop schedules and written procedures.
- Develop/Draft job descriptions for employees.
- Will you use some contract workers?

Inventory

- What kind of inventory will you stock (raw material, finished goods, supplies)?
- Average value of inventory carried (investment).
- What is your projected rate of inventory turnover? How many times purchased inventory is sold? (Cost of Goods relative to Sales; compare to industry average)
- Which inventory items, if any, have seasonal sales?
- What is the lead-time for ordering inventory?

Suppliers (Vendors)

- Names and addresses of major suppliers.
- Type and amount of inventory supplied.
- Policies regarding credit and delivery.
- History and reliability (costs steady or not).
- The need for more than one supplier per item.
- Shortages or delivery problems.

Managing Your Accounts Payable

Explain your Vendors' Credit Terms and your advantages in keeping current with these accounts.

- Cash or Credit purchases.
- What is customary in your industry?
- How will open line purchases be established? (refilling orders of specific products)

- How will your business take advantage of short term payment discounts?
- Planning for "Just in Time" Inventory purchase to conserve cash flow.
- What will be your plan for reviewing aged Accounts Payable?
- What will be your plan for vendor notifications regarding late payments?
- At what point will you ask for extended terms?
- Will you have seasonal cycles in your purchasing of inventories?

Sales Credit Policies

Explain specifically the credit policies you plan on establishing relative to your sales.

- Cash or Credit sales.
- What is customary in your industry?
- Credit limits (minimums and maximums).
- How will Credit Checks be accomplished?
- Terms (discounts for cash or short terms).
- Have you considered and computed your cost for allowing credit?

Managing Your Accounts Receivable

If you do extend credit, explain your plans for checking your aging of open accounts (explain your planned monthly ageing reports from your accounting software).

- What is your Statement Policy? (Monthly, past due, specific age)

- When will you make a phone call?

- When will you send a letter?

- When will you get your attorney involved?

Management and Organization

Explain in detail how individuals will fill the slots in your detailed organizational chart (indicate when you must fill the slot until reaching a certain level).

- Who fills the individual slots (even if it is you in the beginning)?
- Experience each person brings to the business?
- Special or distinctive competencies that person must have.
- Contingency plans if key individuals are incapacitated.
- Include position descriptions for owners and key employees (supply resumes for owners and key employees when a bank loan is involved).

Professional and Advisory Support

Show how you consider your professional and advisory support as part of your overall team.

- Accountant
- Attorney
- Banker
- Insurance Agent
- Consultants
- Management advisory board (key employees)
- Mentors and key advisors
- Board of Directors
- Company Officers

Financial Plan with Projections

When developing the "Financial Plan with Projections", the critical and key projection in the equation is "Sales" (everything revolves around sales).

Be conservative when projecting **"Sales"** (explaining how you arrived at the numbers).

Be liberal when projecting **"Expenses"** also (explaining how you arrived at the numbers).

The Financial Plan consists of the following:

- **12-Month Profit and Loss Projection**

  This is where you put your business plan into action with the numbers relative to; Sales, Cost of Goods, Operating Expenses, Selling Expenses, and Administrative Expenses. This will show how you intend to make your business profitable.

- **Three-Year Profit Projection**

  This is an extension of the "12-Month Profit and Loss Projection" totals, picking up that first year, and adding two additional years. The profit projection is the heart of your business plan.

- **Projected First-Year Cash Flow Statement**

  The point of this worksheet is to plan how much money is needed before startup, for preliminary startup expenses and purchases, Cost of Goods, Operating Expenses, Selling Expenses, Administration Expenses, and Principal Loan payments for the first year of business operations.

- **Projected Three Year Cash Flow Statement**

  This worksheet just extends the Cash Flow to include not only the first year of your business but also the next two years.

If the profit projection is the heart of your Business Plan the cash flow statement is the blood. Businesses fail because they cannot pay their bills. Every part of your business plan is important, but none of it means a thing it you run out of cash.

- **Beginning Balance Sheet**
  This Balance Sheet will reflect how the Assets, Liabilities, and Net Worth appears after applying the original "Start-up" insertion of cash through borrowing (Long Term Debt) or investments (Equity); less the necessary purchases of Inventories and Fixed Assets.
- **Comparative Balance Sheets**
  This Comparative Balance Sheet Report will include the Beginning Balance Sheet plus the Balance Sheets after the three years of operations.

For each of your projections you must explain your major assumptions:

- **Sales & Cost of Goods assumptions**
  Will your Gross Profit be adequate to cover your expenses?
- **Accounts Receivable assumptions**
  Will your collections be timely enough to cover your payment requirements?

- **Loan & Tax Payment assumptions**

  Will your Net Profit be sufficient to cover both your Loan principal and Tax payments?

Personal Financial Statement

Your personal financial statement will indicate to investors and/or lenders the support you will be bringing for the business you are developing. They may require that Personal Financial Statements be supplied for each owner and major stockholders because personal guarantees will more than likely be required.

Your personal financial statement will contain the following information to indicate your ability to support the business venture.

- Assets held outside of this business
- Liabilities owed outside of this business
- Personal Net Worth outside of this business

It is a normal thing for lenders to require a personal guarantee; sometimes even going as far as requiring a second mortgage pledge against your personal residence. Don't show your lack of trust in the success of your business by refusing to pledge your personal residence as collateral.

Capitalization and Startup Expenses

The "Capitalization and Startup Expenses" worksheet will be a part of the Business Plan and will indicate:

- **Capitalization** – the cash, inventory, fixed assets (equipment), and/or supplies you will be inserting in the business originally.
- **Startup Expenses** – is the total amount of cash sufficient to cover expenses for a minimum of one year, additional beginning inventory you need to purchase, and additional fixed assets (equipment) you will need at the beginning. This will be the amount you are seeking from the lender or investor.

Even with the best planning, however; opening a new business has a way of costing more than you anticipate. You must not run out of Cash during that first year therefore it would be prudent to add a separate line item, called Contingencies. Adding a percentage of the budgeted expenses as a contingency fund can protect you and can easily be paid back if you find you don't need it.

Review of Goals for your "Business Plan"

The same key points that were suggested at the end of the Executive Summary are applicable here:

- Make it Enthusiastic and Realistic.
- Make it Professional.
- Make it Complete.
- Make it concise.

Professional Support Team

In conjunction with the development of the Business Plan, the need to consult with the future members of your "Professional Support Team" probably has already occurred.

Questions about the methods of accounting to utilize for your Financial Reports or even assistance in developing "Projected Financial Statements" may have required you to seek the services of an accountant.

Questions about the "Business Structure," purchase or leasing of properties, and contracts may have required you to seek the services of a lawyer.

Questions about working capital needs or long term borrowing may have required you to seek the services of a banker.

Questions about insurance and the cost of insurance packages relative to information you will need for your expense projections may have required you to seek the services of an insurance agent.

The Accountant

Let's start with the "CPA/Accountant" or "Professional Bookkeeper" as our first member of your "Professional Support Team." He is a business advisor who assists the small business owner in the development and implementation of financial plans. For the purposes here, we will refer to him as the "Accountant."

The "Accountant" possesses a wide range of expertise including technical knowledge, business experience, and expertise on business development. An "Accountant" is required to continually update his or her level of knowledge by earning continuing education credits in a variety of subjects.

Many small businesses fail because the owner did not have timely, accurate financial information on which to make intelligent management decisions.

The "Accountant" assists the small business owner by providing the following services:

- **Financial Statement Services**
  o The "Accountant" has the responsibility to teach the small business owner how to read their Financial Statements, keying on the logical footprints.
  o Conducts; audits, reviews, and compilations.
  o Generates regular financial reports based on the owner's needs (monthly, quarterly, or annually) or directed by some outside source.

- o Assists in the analysis of operations including interpretation of financial ratios and development of industry data.
- o Reviews internal controls.

- **Accounting Services**

  Keeping accurate, detailed financial records is very important regardless of the size of a business. The "Accountant" can provide the initial "Bookkeeper" services and assist the small business owner in hiring someone to take care of this function for you on your site.

- **Bookkeeper Services**
  - o Prepare transaction journals.
  - o Posts the General Ledger Reconcile accounts.
  - o Prepares payroll tax and sales tax returns and perform other compliance work.
  - o Maintain depreciation schedules.

- **Management Advisory Services**

  The types of business advisory services may include the following:
  - o Provides assistance in obtaining financing.
  - o Prepares Cash Flow analysis.
  - o Prepares forecasts and projections.
  - o Prepares of budgets.
  - o Provides assistance in preparing a business plan.
  - o Evaluates computer needs and assistance in the selection and implementation of a computer system.

- o Performs business valuations.
- o Analyzes existing general office procedures and recommends improvements.
- o Assists in developing employees benefits plans.
- **Tax Services**
  - o Ever since the first federal tax laws were enacted in 1913, "Accountants" (CPA's) have been extensively involved in tax matters. Because of continual changes in tax laws every CPA must keep abreast of tax matters.
  - o Tax compliance including income tax, payroll tax, sales/use tax, excise and property tax.
  - o Represents clients before the IRS.
  - o Provides Tax planning including options on various transactions, methods for minimizing tax, and depreciation methods/options.
- **Financial Planning Services**
  - o The "Accountant" will assist a business owner with estate planning, retirement planning, and investment alternatives. The "Accountant" provides advice and services including preparation of financial statements, tax planning, compliance work, and management/consulting services.
  - o The "Accountant" is the key for giving the small business manager the initial support needed in the development of their accounting systems; and adequately planning for tax responsibilities.

The Attorney

The "Attorney" is the key for giving the small business person the initial support needed in the development of their corporate structure, both for liabilities and tax planning. Attorneys are becoming specialized more and more as the necessity for more in-depth research is reaching higher levels. The attorney provides a wide range of service and advice:

- Agreements & filing of incorporation papers.
- Partnership agreements.
- Articles of Incorporation.
- Articles of Operating Agreements.
- Basic Zoning compliance.
- Copyright & Trademark, Intellectual Property.
- Negotiate Leases or Purchase Agreements.
- Buy-sell Agreements.
- Software License Agreement.
- Termination of a disruptive Employee.
- Overseeing corporate annual meetings.
- Defense in Lawsuits.
- Contracts.
- Taxes & Licenses.

Business Lawyers may come from large law firms, or smaller firms with specialty practices, from government agencies, within a corporate structure, and even on the staff of large Accounting firms.

The Banker

The Banker is the key for giving the small business manager the initial support in financing the original cash needs for the development of the small business, as well as operating "Lines of Credit."

Having a Personal Business Bank will give you an inside supporter in his bank for needs you request.

- Startup Company needs.
- Short term working capital loans.
- Building and Equipment purchases.
- Long term Loan Structure with custom payback features.
- A representative within the bank to plead your case.
- A sounding board for reviewing Financial Statements.

The Banker probably knows more about you then anyone else on the team. I suggest to the small business community that the businessman with the ability to read and explain his Financial Statements to his Banker will naturally gain more support from him and his bank. The Banker receiving a well explained report regarding the company's financial position will be more open to give that small businessman his banking support.

The Insurance Agent

The Insurance Agent is a valuable team member to assure that the business is adequately protected to withstand outside risks and events and therefore its continuance.

The areas of protection the businessman should request information about are:

- General Liability Insurance
- Automobile Liability Insurance
- Umbrella Liability Insurance
- Workers Compensation Insurance

The key to the financial success of a small business is the team approach; which involves the development of a good "Professional Support Team" in the beginning.

The small business owner should consult with his/her team before the fact – not after the fact!

Chapter Two
General Accounting

This chapter will give you a **practical** overview of **General Accounting** featuring the following very important areas:

- **Chart of Accounts**
- **Financial Statements**
- **Management Footprints/Financial Statement Ratios**
- **Internal Controls**

"Chart of Accounts"

This total listing of accounts is developed to create the accounting paths necessary to provide Financial Statements meaningful to your specific business. This can be accomplished with numbered groups of accounts (both Balance Sheet & Income Statement) pertinent to your business.

"Financial Statements"

They are the economic history reports developed through all of the economic transactions.

"Management Footprints/Ratios"

These are developed by you over a period of time through the study of your small business' Financial Statements and therefore flagging important items.

"Internal Controls"

These are controls established for office procedures; providing protection of company's financial assets. The businessman needs to understand what is necessary to assure internal controls are being maintained by management to safeguard liquid assets.

Chart of Accounts

An **"Account"** (as used in accounting) can best be defined as a "named item" used to record each financial transaction that takes place during an operational period.

> **Balance Sheet** named accounts: each balance sheet named account will either be an Asset, Liability, or an Equity item.

> **Income Statement** named accounts: each income statement named account will either be an Income or Expense item.

The **Chart of Accounts** is a listing of all of the accounts (named items) used in recording the company's historical financial transactions.

The business owner or manager's participation in the development or improvement of the Chart of Accounts will give him/her a much better understanding of the economic operations of their business.

The manager can select key accounts that he wants to glean information from and position them accordingly in the Financial Statements. A good manager can glean a wealth of practical information from a well prepared set of financial statements, utilizing accounts that he/she had input in developing. The numbering system is the key that opens the door for developing and positioning accounts on managerial financial statements.

Numbering System

A three number system is utilized here for simplicity in the examples of the following Balance Sheet and Income Statements accounts. For our purpose here, we will just list the Control Accounts.

Balance Sheet – Key Accounts

Current Assets represent assets that either are already Cash or will become Cash within one year.

100 – Cash on Hand & In Bank

110 – Accounts Receivable

120 – Inventory

130 – Notes Receivable

140 – Prepaid Items

Fixed Assets and Other Assets represents assets with lives longer than one year.

150 – Fixed Assets

160 – Other Assets

Current Liabilities represents liabilities that will come due and must be paid with one year.

200 – Accounts Payable

210 – Notes Payable (short term)

220 – Taxes Payable

230 – Accruals

Long Term Liabilities represents liabilities with payment requirements extending beyond one year.

240 – Notes Payable – Long Term

Equity accounts represent amounts invested by owners and balance of previous plus current year's profit.

300 – Invested Equity

310 – Retained Earnings   (+Current Year Profit)

Income Statement – Key Accounts

The numbering system for the Income Statement has the lowest number in each number group representing the highest level of importance.

400 – Income

As an example - the lowest 400 number usually represents the largest volume item with the balance listed accordingly.

500 – Cost of Goods Sold

The corresponding 500 number for the cost relative to the 400 Sales items (making it very easy to relate cost to sales)

600 – Operating Expenses

This group represents the Cost of Operation expense items (such as Rent & Utilities)

700 – Selling Expenses

This group represents all of the selling expenses and again is listed according to their volume.

800 – Administration Expenses

This group represents all of the expenses relative to the administration & office costs and again is listed according to their volume.

Templates of a Chart of Accounts as well as the Financial Statements are available at the following web site.

http://www.budspracticalaccounting.com

Financial Statements

The Balance Sheet

- The balance sheet is a snap-shot of the company's assets, liabilities, and owner's equity at a particular point in time, and will be different the very next day.

- Usually the Balance Sheet is prepared monthly, quarterly, or annually, and is compared to the Balance Sheet that was prepared at the same point in time the previous year.
- The Balance Sheet tells you the story about what has happened economically to the company.
- The owner/manager can look over the Balance Sheet and have a better understanding of why the accounts are in a certain position on the financial Statement.
- The owner/manager's understanding of the Balance Sheet, and his ability to present it to his banker, will go a long way toward his ability to gain confidence from that banker.
- The Balance Sheet is the Assets you have, the Liabilities you owe, and the Owner's Equity at a set point in time (Assets = Liabilities + Owners Equity. This is the accounting formula).

Income Statement

- The Income Statement reflects the company's operational results for a certain period of time.
- Economic activity should be measured by matching the generated Revenue to matched Expenses for a fixed period of time.
- Historical costs along with Accrual Accounting, allows the businessman to record the transactions relative to that fixed period of time and therefore match generated Revenue with actual Expenses.

- The analysis of the Key Accounts on the Income Statement gives the owner/manager guidance in proper management of his business.
- Accounting should be a strong basic tool for the manager; not something mysterious, and only used for Credit Information.

Cash Flow Statement

The Cash Flow Statement gives the owner/manager the historical sequences of certain things (for a certain period of time) containing the following:

- Revenue and asset changes
- Investment Activities
- Financing Activities

The Cash Flow Statement will tell you where your cash came from and what you spent your cash on; resulting in the balance of Cash at the end of the period.

Management Footprints/Financial Statement Ratios

Balance Sheet Ratios

- The **Current Ratio** is the mathematical relationship of Current Assets to Current Liabilities. By dividing Current Liabilities into Current Assets, the result will show the dollars of Current Assets available to cover Current Liabilities. The goal is to have $2 in Current Assets for every $1 of Current Liabilities (giving you a good liquid Position).

- The **Quick Ratio** is the mathematical relationship of Current Assets minus Inventory (Cash & Accounts Receivable) to Current Liabilities. The question this will answer is how much of the Inventory the owner/manager would need to sell to cover all Current Liabilities.
- The **Inventory Turnover/to Cost of Goods** is the mathematical relationship of how many times the Inventory turns, in relationship to Cost of Goods. This perspective represents the actual number of inventory turns.
- **Accounts Receivable Turnover** is the mathematical relationship of Accounts Receivable to Sales (usually computed as a monthly average). This will give you the results of how long Accounts Receivable would be in house.
- **Debt-to-Equity Ratio** is the mathematical relationship Between Long Term Dept and Owners Equity.

Income Statement Ratios

- Total Revenue is 100% and all expense groups are measured from this base.
- The group's totals become your budget measurements.
- Suggested Groups – (Cost of Goods Group = 500 accounts totals.) (Operating Exp Group = 600 accounts totals.) (Selling Exp Group = 700 accounts totals.) (Administration Exp Group = 800 accounts totals.)

- When you compare your expense percentages as a relative percentage of total revenue you are measuring your effectiveness.
- Example: Cost of Goods Budgeted percentage 40% - actual percentage 41.25% (this would indicate a favorable budget comparison).
- Example: Advertising Budgeted percentage 3% - actual percentage 4% (this would indicate you are over budget for the period measured)
- Owners/Managers trained to review their Financial Statements in this manner will develop their own guideline footprints to look for and therefore enable them to make corrections to their operations quicker.

Internal Controls - (Sensors)

If you consider "Internal Controls" as sensors similar to the warning lights on your car's dashboard (such as Check Engine) you will better understand their purpose.

How can your business establish key sensors (internal controls) to safeguard the handling of funds?

Cash sensors: When funds (money) are used to purchase items, or when funds (money) are received from a customer for a Sale or Service; we need to establish, "Internal Controls"- **sensors**.

Receiving ticket sensors: A policy is established stating that all receiving tickets must be signed, dated, with the item quantity (checked) and item quality (noted). This is a simple rule for the individual receiving items, whether it is an inventory item, a supply item, or a new piece of equipment. A receiving ticket handled in this manner assures that the item was received on the noted date and the quantity/quality received was so noted (the individual that signed the ticket with approval in affect signed the check for payment). The location of the item received may also be noted by the person signing the receiving ticket.

Key receiving ticket sensors:
- Receivers' Signature and Date Received.
- Quantity and Quality of item Received.
- Location of item Received.

Inventory control sensors: The "Inventory Control Sensor" will give us assurances that a system has been established to put a safety net around the inventory items. The "Inventory Control Sensor" will more than likely be a computer generated data entry made at the time the inventory was received. This entry will show that on a specific date in time, x number of items was received, in good condition, and placed in inventory at location y, by warehouseman z.

Now this doesn't totally assure that the item will not walk out of the warehouse, ending up in an employee's car – but the warehouse personnel knows that z signed for the item and put it at location y.

Also, the internal auditing teams can printout the current inventory status report and spot check the items at any time. Individuals on the warehouse team, knowing that the inventory has these "Inventory control sensors," will be more reluctant to take the risk of being caught walking out the door. Example: Pull tickets for inventories pulled out of stock for specific use (production, support, or sales) are inventory sensors.

Small businesses need to establish regular times for physical inventories (monthly, quarterly, semi-annually, or annually). They also need to make random, "surprise" physical inventories of key inventory items where the warehousemen have no idea of the timing of this physical inventory.

Key Inventory Control sensors:
- Data entry for Inventory Received.
- Pull ticket for inventories movements.

Cash/Accounts Receivable Sensors: A specific Accounts Receivable Clerk assigned for the Credit Sales data entry; a separate Cash Receipts Clerk to record the payments received from customers; and finally a different clerk responsible to taking the cash receipts to the bank.

Since data entry reports are generated along the way you can see that this internal control "Accounts Receivable Sensors" protects the money flow, making it more difficult to abscond with the funds.

Key Accounts Receivable Sensors:
- Accounts Receivable Clerk recording the sale.
- Cash Receipts Clerk recording cash received.
- Someone else making the actual bank deposit.

Payment/Accounts Payable Sensors: A specific Accounts Payable Clerk assigned to recording invoices received for payment; a separate individual responsible for pulling all invoices for payment, and preparing the check for payment (this same individual will attach all invoices to checks written and pass the group of checks along for signature). The person or persons with check signing authority will review the attached invoices to assure that proper payments are being made. The person signing the checks should either mail the checks, or at least have someone other than the original person who prepared the checks take care of the mailing.

Key Accounts Payable Sensors:
- One person bundles invoices and checks.
- Authorized signatures for all checks.

Payroll Sensors: A Payroll Clerk will prepare all of the time sheets for the payroll requiring authorized initials by supervisors for overtime and special pay situations. Again, an authorized check-signer will review the payroll attachments to assure that the "Payroll Sensors" are in place. A supervisory capacity individual will pass out the payroll checks to keep the arms length control over individuals paid.

Key Payroll Sensors:

- Payroll Clerk accumulates time sheets.
- Authorized initials for overtime.
- Authorized signatures for all checks.
- Supervisory individual to hand out checks.

Fixed Asset Sensors: I recommend that a good internal control system for Fixed Assets is the development of Fixed Asset Worksheets that are brought up to date immediately after their purchase. If you start this Fixed Asset Worksheet in the beginning it will be a routine thing to do and give you a valuable data source for computing depreciation and amortization; as well as assuring that Fixed Assets are protected with insurance. Have a separate section on the worksheet for each Fixed Asset Group: Buildings, Machinery & Equipment, Office Furniture, Fixtures, & Equipment, Leasehold Improvements, and Land.

The Fixed Asset Worksheets become the separate sensors that tie all fixed asset purchases to the General Ledger (By: Type of Fixed Asset, date purchased, cost, estimated life, depreciation)

Summary of "Internal Control" factors you should keep in mind as a small business owner.

- If you consider "Internal Control" items as *sensors* (similar to the sensors you see on your car's dashboard) you will better understand their purpose.

- "Internal Control Sensors" help to make sure that the business receives all of its income; without any of it being siphoned off by waste, fraud, dishonest employees or just carelessness.

- It is a good idea to establish an "Internal Control" Manual that will list all of the **Policies and Procedures** you have established for each "Internal Control Sensor."

- Review your "Internal Control Manual" with your outside accountant to get his input regarding your coverage of "Internal Controls."

- Once you have your "Internal Control System" in place you can fine-tune it by controlling the more obvious weaknesses that appear.

- The Key to a good working "Internal Control System" is the "Segregation of Duties" to assure that one individual doesn't control the individual function from beginning to end.

Chapter Three
Legal

By

Darrell K. Stock

Darrell Stock, is a practicing attorney, and will present this chapter on "Legal Needs of Small Businesses." Darrell has been a workshop presenter for the Lincoln SCORE Chapter for over 25 years relative to his desire to help small businesses have a better understanding of their legal needs and requirements.

Darrell earned his BA from the University of Nebraska in 1972 and his Juris Doctorate from the University of Nebraska in 1974. He is a member of the "Nebraska Bar Association" and the "Nebraska Association of Trial Attorneys." The General Litigation he covers includes the following: Contract Disputes, Evictions, Estate Disputes, Negligence Matters, Insurance Disputes, and Commercial and Private Business Disputes. In the field of Business Law his coverages include: Formation of Corporations, Shareholder Agreements, Limited Liability Companies, Family Limited Partnerships, Real Estate Contacts, Leases, Sale or Purchase Business Agreements, Liquor License Matters, and Hotel Law.

Establishing an Attorney/Client Relationship

In seeking to establish an attorney/client relationship with an attorney for your business, there are a number of attributes which you will want to keep in mind. Are business matters a regular part of their practice? Are you able to establish good communication with the attorney and are they accessible? For some businesses it is important that the attorney have experience in your industry as specialized issues may arise. Since many of the issues on which you will be seeking advice involve litigation, or possible future litigation, it is important that your attorney either be experienced in litigation, or has access to an experienced litigator.

Choosing an Attorney

The main problem for a client in choosing an attorney is that in most states there exists no process for certifying the attorney as experienced and/or competent in any given area. The reality is that just because an attorney lists a specialty in his or her advertisement, it does not mean that they have the requisite experience and competency in that area. Because there is almost no regulation of this advertising, an attorney can list areas in which they have little experience.

The most reliable method for choosing an attorney is by obtaining a referral from your accountant, banker, insurance agent, or other people you know in business. You may want to also consult with individuals who are in the same industry for a recommendation.

Your goal should be that the person making the referral or recommendation has a sufficient amount of experience with the attorney to determine whether or not the attorney is competent in the area of business, their billings are reasonable, and the attorney gets the work in a timely manner. In most instances, it is the accountant who is in the best position to have had experience with a variety of attorneys regarding those attributes.

Ultimately, and most importantly, you will need to choose an attorney with whom you feel comfortable and feel you are able to communicate effectively.

Attorney's Fees

The arrangement where clients paid an attorney in advance to "retain them" is generally a thing of the past. Currently, when an attorney is "retained", it is more about whether or not the client and attorney believe that there is an ongoing attorney/client relationship. The more common arrangement today is that the attorney bills the client for the actual time spent on matters for the client, including the occasional phone calls.

Intellectual Property

Intellectual property law has become a specialty and it is highly likely that the attorney who is appropriate for you may have to refer you to another attorney who specializes in intellectual property law for issues involving trade names, trademarks, service marks and patents.

Company Structure

Sole Proprietorship

This is by far the most common form of "Company Structure" as it is the normal starting point for most small businesses. The owner has the total responsibility and liability for everything connected with the company and will report the Profit or Loss on his personal income tax return. Since he/she is the company – the company dies when the owner dies, which can end up a problem if special a special license or permits is required. The owner's do not draw a paycheck and normally would withdraw funds in the form of a draw.

- The business is literally an extension of you as an individual owner. You can use a trade name and hire employees and agents.
- The sole proprietor receives all the profits of the business and bears all the burdens, including sole responsibility for losses.
- The business cannot outlive the sole proprietor.
- The sole proprietor has unlimited liability for all obligations incurred in doing business
- The sole proprietor pays personal income taxes on profits of the business.
- There are few legal formalities.

Partnership

This is an alternative to a sole proprietorship when two or more individuals join together to own and operate a business. A partnership can be formed by a "handshake" or by a written agreement. Again, when one of the partners dies the partnership ceases to exist. A separate partnership return must be filed and the individual partners will include their share of the income on their personal tax return.

The biggest risk in a partnership is that each partner is responsible for all of the partnership debt and a liability created by one partner can cause all of the partners to be equally liable for debts of the partnership. Partnership agreements must cover all responsibilities.

- A partnership consists of two or more parties.
- Partnership profits or losses are pooled and either shared equally or distributed as stated in the partnership agreement.
- The life of a partnership is relative to the lifespan of any one partner, or until one partner sells his or her share (per their original partnership agreement).
- Each partner may be individually liable for any partnership debts or liabilities caused by the action of any other partner.
- Share of controls of the partnership is dependent upon the original partnership agreement.

Corporation

Individuals can decide to legally establish their "Company Structure" as a corporation through filing the necessary forms through an attorney. Their attorney and accountant will advise the owners the legal requirements for their state as well as the related tax consequences.

- Exists as a separate entity, an intangible being separate from its shareholders, even if there is only one shareholder.
- Each state through their Secretary of State must approve the creation of each corporation.
- Yearly payment of Corporation Occupation Tax is required to keep the corporation legitimately alive.
- The structure of a corporation requires the "Articles of Incorporation" and the by-laws and must operate within these rules and regulations.
- Regular corporate meetings are required.
- The corporation is legally responsible for its debts and obligations, as well as the actions of its shareholders, officers, directors, and employees.
- A shareholder has limited liability and the maximum loss is the investment.
- Officers upon co-signing or giving a personal guarantee will lose their limited liability.
- The corporation must file its own tax return.
- A corporation may elect to file as a "Sub S" where gains or losses flow to the shareholders.

Limited Liability Company

The "Limited Liability Company" is an alternative to a partnership and has very similar characteristics to it, in addition to some of the characteristics of a corporation. The structure of the "Limited Liability Company" is supported by "Articles of Organization" which would be considered similar to the "Articles of Incorporation" in a "Corporation" structure.

The internal operating rules are set forth in an "Operating Agreement" which is the equivalent of "Bylaws" for a corporation.

The driving reasons for formation of this form of "Company Structure" are the limited liability and the pass-through income tax angle. The LLC can make their choice of tax regime. An LLC can elect to be taxed as a sole proprietor, partnership, S corporation or C corporation, providing for a great deal of flexibility, but such choice should be made only after consulting with your attorney and tax consultant.

- LLC's are established and operated according to the state laws and statutes.
- Registration and payment of fees is made through the Secretary of State where founded.
- The LLC requires a filed "Articles of Organization."
- The LLC has the advantage of the same flexibility relative to income taxes as a partnership as well as the limited liability of corporations.

- The "Operating Agreement" in an LLC is equivalent of "Bylaws" for a corporation.

In conclusion, the choices for whichever "Company Structure" you select for your company should be made only after consulting with your attorney and tax consultant.

Chapter Four
Financing

By

Jim Mastera

Jim Mastera, a retired banker, who spent his banking career with Cornhusker Bank, Lincoln, Nebraska will present this chapter on "Financing Your Small Business." He served as Executive Vice President with emphasis on general management and commercial lending. For many years, Jim has made presentations to a variety of organizations and groups regarding the lending process. (These include the Ks-Ne Schools of Banking, American Institute of Banking, and SCORE) He has frequently been a guest speaker at Nebraska Wesleyan University and Doane College. His educational background includes both a BA and MAA from Doane College as well as Graduate Degree from the Colorado School of Banking.

The goal of this chapter is to provide you with a better understanding of financing your business enterprise. Your small business needs for financing may occur as you are beginning the business and may continue during the life of your business. You may need to borrow for start-up costs and you may also need to borrow to finance inventory, receivables, asset purchases, or working capital needs. Your lender will require certain information from you to put this borrowing in place.

What a Lender Needs to Know:

1. About You

The assumption by the lender is that you, as an individual, are an integral part of your small business. You and the business basically are one and the same. As a result, the lender will require information about you personally regarding management ability and financial responsibility.

Management of a small business is the key to success. You will need to provide the lender assurance of your management skills. Your past history may be an indicator of your abilities. Providing a resume that defines your past experience will give definition to your ability to manage your small business. Your resume should indicate that you have the background to do what you intend to do in your business.

The lender will rely heavily on your credit ability or credit worthiness. You will be asked to provide personal financial documents (such as balance statement and either income statement or copy of your tax return). The two pieces of information provide two different pieces of information about you personally.

The balance sheet indicates your net worth (total assets less total debt) on the day of the preparation of the statement the assumption is that if you sold everything, paid off all debt, the net worth is the remaining value that you provide. The income statement or personal tax return will each provide a picture of your income or earning capacity for a given time period, typically on an annual basis. This information provides information on repayment ability.

Credit Bureau report and references also provide a history of how you have paid other creditors. A positive credit history is a necessity for future borrowing. Credit references may be the same as listed on the credit bureau report, but may also include other sources that are not bureau reported, such as utility payments, rental payments, etc.

2. About Your Business

The lender will require financial information about your business much the same as provided on your personally, and for the same reasons, to assess your ability to repay the loan.

The following are examples of the reports that will be required.

Balance Sheet

This is a listing of the "business" assets, debt and net worth. This report details the net value of the business, commonly referred to as capital.

Income Statement

The income statement is a record of the revenue less all expenses of the business during a period of time. These may be monthly, quarterly or annually.

Cash Flow Statement

The cash flow statement provides information on the amount of cash available from your business operation to repay your loan or loans.

3. **Projection**

Projecting the financial outcome of your business operations is also necessary in the borrowing process. Basically, this can be considered a budget. It is important as it gives an indication of your thoughts regarding the operation of your business.

Typically a projection will never be exact. Rather, it provides the mechanism for you to know and understand the financial workings of your business as well as to demonstrate this knowledge to your lender.

Over time, you will be asked to provide all of these reports to the lender. This will provide an ongoing financial history of your company that will be used by the lender to compare actual results to your projections, define trends occurring in the business, and to predict the financial future of the business.

4. Financing Needs

Your loan request should detail how much you need to borrow, what the loan proceeds will be used for, term and structure of repayment, and sources of funds for repayment.

There are many reasons to borrow and each of them may require specific repayment terms. For example, vehicles or equipment may need to be financed over a longer period of time as opposed to inventory, which may require a shorter period of time for repayment. Borrowing needs may incorporate one or more of these needs, but the loans should be specific to the need.

5. Collateral Pledging

You will be asked to provide a listing of collateral to secure your loan. Collateral can be tangible assets such as real estate, vehicles, equipment, furniture/fixtures and inventory as well as intangibles such as contract rights, accounts and insurance cash value. Collateral if required to mitigate the risk of non-payment of the loan.

6. Other Information

A cosigner may at times be necessary to obtain a loan. The cosigner must provide financial strength when it is not available from the business owners. A cosigner will be required to provide all financial information that is required of the loan applicant.

The financial information that is required by the lender is itemized to give a complete understanding of the financial standing of the small business. This same information should also provide the same understanding to the small business owner/loan applicant. A thorough understanding of the financial standing of the company will help the owner to better manage the business.

Chapter Five
Insurance

By

Rich Oehlerking

Rich Oehlerking, a retired insurance agent, will share his knowledge of this industry regarding where the "Risks" of operating a business are covered.

Rich graduated from Ogallala, Nebraska high school and received his BSBA from the University of Nebraska. The first five years of his working life was spent as a manager for the Singer Company.

He started his career in the field of insurance in 1962 and continued in his chosen profession until his retirement in 2001. Rich started as a Producer, worked his way up to Founder/Producer, and spent his last five years as a Consultant/Partner.

Rich was involved with Jaycees, the Nebraska Chapter of Chartered Property & Casualty Underwriters, Independent Insurance Agents of Lincoln, on the Governor's Committee to Reorganize Workers' Compensation-Nebraska, was the Chairman of the Lincoln SCORE Chapter, and is still involved with SCORE both as a volunteer and as a workshop presenter (insurance of course).

Rich's chapter on insurance follows the same type of format that he uses in his SCORE workshop presentation, and I'm sure will be very helpful in giving the reader a basic understanding of the five basic insurance topics covered.

1. General Liability Insurance
2. Automobile Liability Insurance
3. Umbrella Liability Insurance
4. Workers Compensation Insurance

General Liability Insurance

When a person goes into business, they generally create an "entity" which did not previously exist (Sole Proprietorship, Partnership, Corporation, or Limited Liability Company).

The entity is "liable" for the errors and torts which it might commit through its day-to-day operation. Such acts might cause injury to or damage persons or property that belongs to others.

Coverage for such potential (or actual) damage or injury can be provided by purchasing a **Comprehensive General Liability Policy.** Such a policy is written to cover acts or omissions which cause injury or damage to persons or property belonging to others.

(Certain Insurance Companies may develop other names for their policies, but will know that this general title is that which provides coverage.)

Such a policy should be written to provide, **"Bodily Injury and Property Damage" limits of $1,000,000 for "Each Occurrence" and $2,000,000 "Aggregate."**

(Lower limits are, of course, available, but the person or business obtaining such coverage will find that lower limits save very little. Remember, "Don't risk a lot to save a little")

"Bodily Injury" provides coverage for injuries that a person might incur.

"Property Damage" provides coverage for property belonging to persons other than the "Named Insured" named on the policy.

(Various insurance companies may use different titles to describe their policies of this type, but their agents should be able to explain that their form follows under this General Liability Insurance title.)

Automobile Liability Insurance

An Automobile Liability policy may also provide a section for the **"Physical Damage"** of the vehicles listed on the policy. *(Generally known as Collision and Comprehensive)*

More importantly, it also provides coverage for **"Bodily Injury Liability"** and **"Property Damage Liability."** These coverages operate like the liability sections of the General Liability Policy mentioned above and provide coverage for the "Named Insured" and other "Insured parties" (like employees) who might cause injury or damage to property (including vehicles) belonging to others arising out of the use of an insured motor vehicle.

Limits under this policy for Liability (for damages arising out of the usage of a "motor vehicle") should be written at **$1,000,000 per occurrence – or above.**

Umbrella Liability Insurance

If limits of liability higher than those listed on the three liability policies listed above are desired or necessary, a coverage widely known as an **"Umbrella"** can (and probably should be) obtained.

This type of policy can provide additional liability protection where the limits on the above liability policies are not adequate (or "prudent"). Additional limits in increments of **$1,000,000** – which applies in addition to the coverages provided by the above policies can be obtained.

Workers Compensation Insurance

This is the only coverage actually required by State Law in Nebraska (and nearly every other state.

State Law requires that any business which has *"any employee(s)"* must purchase (and keep in force) a Workers Compensation Insurance policy. The Workers Compensation Insurance policy provides coverage for all valid and reasonable medical expenses resulting from an on-the-job injury. If the injured person is off work more than (8) days, this coverage will pay 66 2/3% of their wages up to a Maximum of $710 weekly *(this limit is up-dated annually)*.

The second section of a Workers Compensation Insurance policy provides a limit for **"Employers' Liability"** which coverage comes into effect if an injured employee elects to "sue" the employer rather than take "guaranteed" coverage under the first section of the policy.

Chapter Six
Government

1. What is Government?

2. The Structure of Taxes

3. Checklist for Starting a Business

4. Excess Government Regulations

What is Government?

In the case of its broad definition, government normally consists of legislators, administrators, and arbitrators. Government is the means by which state policy is enforced, as well as the mechanism for determining the policy of the state. A form of government, or form of state governance, refers to the set of political institutions by which a government of a state is organized.

The Constitution of the United States covers areas very important to the small business owner. Understand the connection for your business.

The Constitution of the United States –

We the People of the United States, in order to form a more perfect Union, establish Justice, insure domestic Tranquility, provide of the common defence, promote the general Welfare, and secure the Blessings of Liberty to ourselves and our Posterity, do ordain and establish this Constitution for the United States Of America.

- ### Article 1 – Section 1

All legislative Powers herein granted shall be vested in a Congress of the United States, which shall consist of a Senate and House of Representatives.

- ### Article 1 – Section 7

All Bills for raising Revenue shall originate in the House of Representatives; but the Senate may propose or concur with Amendments as on other Bills.

- ### Article 1 – Section 8

The Congress shall have Power to lay and collect Taxes, Duties, Imposts and Excises, to pay the Debts and provide for the common Defence and general Welfare of the United States; but all Duties, Imposts and Excises shall be uniform throughout the United States

Article 1 - Section 8 mentions the following relative to businesses: to borrow money, to regulate Commerce (with foreign Nations and among the several States), to establish a uniform Rule of Naturalization and uniform laws on the subject of Bankruptcies throughout the United States, to coin Money, regulate the Value thereof, and fix the Standard of Weights and Measures, and to provide for the Punishment of counterfeiting.

This information shows the close ties small business has to principles found in our Constitution. Congress was established not to run our small business but to protect their rights. States cannot impose Tax or Duty on Articles exported from businesses in their states (this being uniform across the United States protecting the small business).

The goal for business owners should be to elect members to Congress that will not only protect individual rights but the rights as owners of our small businesses.

When we find that members of Congress are imposing a *"Structure of Taxes"* or *"Excess Government Regulations"* that is a hardship for individuals or their businesses to proceed successfully they should be replaced with members who are willing to uphold our Constitution and the Rights of individuals.

The Structure of Taxes

Tax forms Required for each Company Structure
Sole Proprietor
File a Schedule C for the business, along with your personal 1040 form (Due April 15th each year)

Partnership
The partnership files Form 1065, which includes a schedule K-1 stating the share of partnership income and seductions for each partner. (Form 1065 is due April 15th each year) (Schedule K-1 is sent to each partner for filing with their 1040 by April 15th)

LLC
With one owner, you follow the rules for a sole proprietorship. If there are two or more owners, follow the rules for a partnership. (Two or more owner LLCs can elect to file as a Sub S Corporation)

Sub S Corporation
File Form 1120S, whether you have one or more owners. (The return is due March15) At that time, you must also provide each owner with a Schedule K-1 showing the share of corporate income and deductions for each owner.

C Corporation
File Form 1120, whether you have one or more owners. (The return is due March 15) There are no Schedule K-1 requirements for a C Corporation.

How you personally report income and expenses

Sole Proprietor & One-person LLC

Pays tax on profits &/or losses from the business on a personal return.

Owners/Partners, LLC Members, & S Corp shareholders

Pay tax on their share of business income &/or losses on their personal returns.

C Corporations are separate taxpayers

They are taxed on their profits and can deduct losses, subject to certain limits.

Owners of C Corporations

Only pay tax on their personal returns on salary, dividends and other taxable amounts distributed to them.

Social Security & Medicare Taxes (FICA)

If you work for your corporation, S or C, and receive a salary, FICA is levied only on your salary (not on the profits).

Self-employed individuals (sole proprietors, partners and LLC members) are subject to self-employment tax on their net earnings (namely all profits). This self-employment tax is made up of both the employee and employer share of FICA taxes.

Make Tax Planning Decisions Early

Your Audit Risk is Increased
You increase your odds for an audit by the IRS If you are a (sole proprietor, partner, or a one person LLC member).

Know how to maximize your business expenses
In general – All the ordinary and necessary expenses paid or incurred during the taxable year in carrying on any trade or business shall be allowed as a business deduction.

Personal Expense Flags by IRS
The number one concern of the IRS when auditing business deductions is whether purely personal expenditures are being claimed as business expenses (such as: cost of commuting to work, using a business credit card for a vacation, or excess pay to family).

Checklist for Starting a Business

When starting a small business check the government regulations, both state and national. They will have a checklist of items that you will need to do first. Check with the United States Internal Revenue Department and your Secretary of State to make sure you are covering all requirements. The following is a basic check list for your use, but you may need to add to this list if changes occur.

1. **Choose a name:**

   Choose a name that is unique, creative, and suits your business. Once you have a number of options, check with the Secretary of State to determine whether your choices are available in your state. If you are going to create a web site it is advisable to check website name availability.

2. **Determine your business address:**

   In order to file most entity and licensing related documents you will need to establish a street address, in most cases a PO Box is not sufficient. Remember, the business address you select and use on government forms will become public record.

3. **Choose your business entity:**

   As we discussed earlier, you more than likely will consult your accountant and attorney as to the best choice of entity for your business.

4. **Apply for an EIN number:**

   An Employer Identification Number (EIN), also known as a Federal ID, is to a business what a social security number is to an individual. You can operate as a sole proprietorship and use your social security number, but if your business has more than one owner, you will definitely want to use an EIN.

5. **Register with your State Department of Revenue:**

   As an example, if you are starting a new business in Nebraska, you need to register with the Nebraska Department of Revenue. In Nebraska registration is required if you have employees, intend to engage in retail sales, renting/leasing personal property, or will be providing services which are subject to sales tax. Check with your own state to see what their requirements are.

6. **Apply for a Business License & Necessary Permits:**

   Depending upon the products and services you intend to provide, you may need to apply for and receive a business license. Again, check with your own state to see what their requirements are. In Nebraska some of the businesses with licensing requirements are construction contractors, massage therapists, insurance and real estate agents and day care providers. Building permits may also be required.

Excess Government Regulations

When government regulations relative to small businesses reach beyond what is reasonable and prudent our economy will suffer and our small businesses will have problems passing their costs on to the consumer.

The Heritage Foundation is an institution that was founded as a watchdog for us to assure that excess government regulations are brought to light and therefore will protect all Americas Small Businesses, by making known these excesses.

The Heritage Foundation

Founded in 1973, The Heritage Foundation is a research and educational institution—a think tank—whose mission is to formulate and promote conservative public policies based on the principles of free enterprise, limited government, individual freedom, traditional American values, and a strong national defense.

We believe the principles and ideas of the American Founding are worth conserving and renewing. As policy entrepreneurs, we believe the most effective solutions are consistent with those ideas and principles. Our vision is to build an America where freedom, opportunity, prosperity, and civil society flourish.

Economic freedom is the liberty to make full use of one's property rights in open and free markets. It protects the right to freely produce, exchange, distribute, and consume goods and services without coercion or constraint beyond what is necessary to protect and maintain liberty.

At home, economic freedom protects the free movement of labor, the right to enjoy the fruit of one's labors, and the right to acquire, own, use, and sell property as one chooses. Governments have a duty to protect these rights with settled, known laws, impartial judges, and enforcement mechanisms.

Many small business owners support **The Heritage Foundation** by becoming a member. Through membership they will receive their research data, keeping them informed and aware of what is happening in our government. The reports and articles that are made available will keep them on top of items that can greatly affect small businesses.

As an example; The Heritage Foundation submitted an article written by James Gattuso and Diane Katz – December 28, 2012 – that brings to light "the 10 worst regulations of 2012."

Morning Bell: The 10 Worst Regulations of 2012

It seems that no aspect of American life can escape government regulation. In the past year, regulators drafted rules that addressed everything from caloric intake to dishwasher efficiency.

Most of these rules increase the cost of living, others hinder job creation, and many erode freedom. Not all regulations are unwarranted, of course, but increasingly, the rules imposed by the government or individuals get to make basic pocketbook and lifestyle decisions that affect them. And it is not just the regulators who are to blame. Congress writes laws that give unelected bureaucrats the broad powers they wield.

1. **HHS's Contraception Mandate**

   The Department of Health and Human Services on February 15 finalized its mandate that *all* health insurance plans include coverage for (abortion-inducing drugs, sterilization procedures, and contraceptives). To date, *42 cases with more than 110 plaintiffs* are challenging this restriction on religious liberty.

2. **EPA Emissions Standards**

   The EPA in February finalized strict new *emissions standards for coal – and oil-fired electric utilities.* The benefits are highly questionable, with the vast majority being unrelated to the emissions targeted by the regulation. The costs, however, are certain: an estimated $9.6 billion annually.

3. **Fuel Efficiency Standards**

   In August, the National Highway Traffic Safety Administration, in tandem with the Environmental Protection Agency, finalized *fuel efficiency standards for cars and light trucks* for model years 2017-2025. The rules require a whopping average fuel economy of 54.5 miles per gallon by 2025. Sticker prices will jump by hundreds of dollars.

4. New York's 16-Ounce Soda Limit

Not all regulations come from Washington. On September 13, at the behest of Mayor Michael Bloomberg, the New York City Board of Health *banned the sale of soda and other sweetened drinks* in containers larger than 16 ounces.

5. Dishwasher Efficiency Standards

Regulators admit that these Department of Energy rules will do little to improve the environment. Rather, proponents claim they will save consumers money. They will also increase the price of dishwashers, and only about one in sic consumers will keep his or her dishwasher long enough to *recoup the cost.*

6. School Lunch Standards

The U.S. Department of Agriculture in January published *stringent nutrition standards for school lunch and breakfast programs.* More than 98,000 elementary and secondary schools are affected – at a cost exceeding $3.4 billion over the next four years.

7. Quickie Union Election Rule

In April, the National Labor Relations Board issued new rules that shorten the time allowed for union-organizing elections to between 10 and 21 days.

This leaves *little time for employees to make a fully informed choice* on unionizing, threatening to leave workers and management alike under unwanted union regimes.

8. **Essential Benefits Rule**

Under Obamacare, insurers in the individual and small group markets will be forced to cover services that the *government deems to be essential.* Published on November 26, the HHS list of very broad benefits has created enormous uncertainty about the extent of essential treatment.

9. **Electronic Data Recorder Mandate**

The National Highway Traffic Safety Administration on December 13 issued a notice of proposed rulemaking to mandate installation of electronic data recorders, popularly known as *"black boxes,"* in most light vehicles starting in 2014. The government mandate understandably spooks privacy advocates.

10. **Simplified Mortgage Disclosure and Servicing**

In July, the Consumer Financial Protection Bureau released its proposal for a more *"consumer friendly"* mortgage process, with a stated goal of simplifying home loans. The rules run an *astonishing 1,099 pages.* Then, one month later, the bureau proposed more than 560 pages of rules for mortgage servicing.

The small business owner cannot be passive when it comes to what is happening to our small businesses, and your membership in The Heritage Foundation will keep you informed. By being a better informed businessman you can alert your representatives in Congress as to what your needs for protection of your rights are.

Chapter Seven
Leadership

By

Ed Nix

Ed Nix wrote this chapter on Leadership because of his experience in the field as well as him becoming a John Maxwell Team Certified Coach/Trainer and Speaker. John Maxwell is well known for his books on Leadership. Ed had a very humble entrepreneurial quest at the ripe old age of 8, in 1960, as a 'Shoe Shine Boy' on the south side of Chicago. He advised me that he learned a lot about perseverance, sales, and customer service working at this first job. He graduated from Illinois State University with honors in 1977 thanks to the G.I. Bill. In 1978 he got his first 'career' position with a large international company, progressing through the ranks and achieving a level of Senior Operations Manager for Europe. He managed a $7 million contract in London England with 486 employees. After serving his time in London he returned to Lincoln, NE where he purchased a small (13 employee) cleaning business in 1990. He sold that same business in 2009 (which had achieved a level of 180 employees), and had increased revenue from $200,000 to $3 million. During his last year of ownership he was employed as a full time consultant in Bangalore, India. A neat experience for a Shoe Shine Boy!

This Leadership Chapter is here to give you a reference for understanding these basic ideas, giving you an opportunity to start leadership development from the beginning. Having someone present Leadership in this manner allows you to not only gain a better understanding but to have a better pattern to work toward.

Leadership is my passion. I have always loved leadership, I've spent most of my life in leadership positions, and quite frankly I agree with my mentor John Maxwell that "Everything rises and falls on Leadership."

Leadership is a key part of any business if it is to be successful. All businesses have a mission. Some want to make the world a better place for all of us, some want to radically change how we accomplish things that make our lives better by introducing new products and others seek to provide much needed services. Businesses need to accomplish their mission, and leadership is the vehicle of forward motion toward the mission... Ed Nix

**Mission is about what,
Vision is about where,
Values are about why.**

O K, you might say, "So, what is this leadership thing that I need?"

Let me start by telling you what leadership is NOT.

- **Leadership is not management-**

  There are significant differences in the two. Think about yourself. Do you like to be managed? Probably not, when people are managed they usually feel "micro-managed." Systems, budgets, programs, and paperwork gets managed; people get led.

- **Leadership is not position-**

  Many leaders have a position such as CEO, COO, President, etc. The truth is that a position is not necessary for one to lead, and it also is not a guarantee that one will be the leader if he/she has a position. There are many instances where leaders have come to the forefront with a position at all. Martin Luther King led the Civil Rights movement without a designated position.

- **Leadership is not title-**

  Much like position, many leaders have a title, but it is not necessary and it certainly does not guarantee that people will follow. Many people have great titles and nobody following them. An absolute requirement of leadership is that someone is following!

- **Leadership is not power-**

  Power can move people, but it will only last for short periods of time, and will not work once it has stopped being used. Often real leaders have no power. I think of Mother Theresa. She had no title, no position, and no power, yet she was a world class leader.

Leadership Influence

Again, I find myself in total agreement with John Maxwell, "Leadership is influence, nothing more, nothing less."

- **Leaders influence people.**

    Leadership is about influencing team mates, superiors, subordinates, customers and suppliers.

    It is even about influencing yourself. The single biggest challenge of my life has been self leadership. I believe that is true for many of us. It is also the key to further growth in leadership. How can you expect to lead others if you wouldn't even follow yourself? As we proceed through this chapter I will further explain 'self leadership' as the place to start your leadership journey.

What Leadership is About

- **Leadership is all about people.**

    It is the art of getting people to go where they might not otherwise go for the purpose of being blessed in a way that they probably did not expect.

    Leadership in the context of this book is primarily aimed at achieving desirable business goals. When employees follow effective business leaders the rewards accrue to the entire company. When companies do well, there are usually greater opportunities for the employees.

- **Leadership is about Mission.**

  Leadership always occurs in the context of mission. The leader is responsible for accomplishing a pre-determined goal or set of goals. Relationships are formed and developed between followers and leaders for the specific purpose of some identifiable mission. It usually is not a matter of just becoming friends.

- **Leadership is about Vision.**

  The leader casts a vision of the final destination that the journey is designed to lead to. In the military, it might be the capturing of a hill. In business it can be the acquiring of a specific market share or status within the market. It is the leader's job to develop and transmit the vision of where the team is going. Mission is about what is to be done, and vision is about where are we going.

- **Leadership is about Values.**

  It is the responsibility of the leader to outline the values of the team, and ensure that there is a 'values match' of the followers. The issue of values is to ensure that all of the members of the team are on the same page.

If the mission is to 'win', and the vision is to be the 'national champions', there is probably a value to 'compete'. If a team member has no value for competition, it is the leader's role to remove him/her from the team. Obviously, the person will inhibit the accomplishment of the team mission and vision.

What Do Leaders Do?

- **Leaders develop positive relationships with people.**
  This is a main activity of those who seek to lead. Without a solid foundation of relationship, people will not follow.
- **Equipping people for success is a primary function of the leader.**
  Equipping can include training, providing material, establishing processes, encouraging, teaching, and removing obstacles from the path of the follower. Leaders that understand the need to equip others, and are able to prepare themselves to perform that function, will enhance their leadership ability and the ability of their followers. Equipping is always a process. One training program is not enough to prepare a person for success in most situations. Effective leaders understand that the process of equipping and developing team members is a fluid process. While there are definite goals and strategies, equipping requires flexibility in method and timing so that adjustments can be made to facilitate the most effective learning outcomes of each team member.
- **Leaders inspire and motivate others to follow.**
  Successful leaders understand that different people are motivated and inspired in different ways. It is rare that an entire team of people will respond to the same motivation in the same way. What inspires one person may not inspire others.

It is incumbent upon the leader to know and respond to each of his followers in a way that works. Managers often treat people the same while good leaders realize that they must treat people differently.

- **Rewards and recognition are tools in the leader's tool box.**

    The leader is required to use rewards and recognition in a way that benefits the mission of the organization while maximizing the loyalty and performance of the team members. Judicious use of rewards will demonstrate fairness to team members. It is important that the leader recognize team members for their effort and reward those that are performing above and beyond the requirement. Care should be taken to ensure that the rewards given to one team member aren't a source of angst for other team members. When team members are giving their best effort and not achieving the goal, the leader must encourage them with sincere recognition.

- **Developing teams as well as team members is a key to good leadership.**

    Obviously the leader needs to grow the team members and equip them to fulfill the mission. The leader also must deploy the team members in the positions where they will be most effective. Developing the team as a working unit demands that each member be placed in a position that utilizes their strengths for the best benefit of the team.

Organizing the members around the specific mission using their individual and collective strengths and abilities is no small matter for the leader. This process will take time and practice to get it right.

- **Good Leaders earn the trust and respect of those that they lead.**

  A big contributor to earning the respect and trust of followers is when the leader *exemplifies the values* that the organization stands for. When team members do not respect the leader, they follow reluctantly. When they don't trust the leader, they will question his/her leadership. When follower's minds are occupied by questioning the leader, less than optimal dedication to the mission is guaranteed.

- **Leaders use, submit to, and share power.**

  Good leaders are good followers. No leader is above all others. Leaders often use power. If they rely on power too heavily, it will undermine their leadership ability. Influence is always preferable to power. Leadership demands that we submit to the power of others and that we submit to the rules of the organization. Failure to do so will undoubtedly undermine a leader's credibility. In most situations the leader is part of a *'Leadership Team'*. It is paramount that he/she shares power and authority with that leadership team. Anytime a leader becomes disassociated with his peers he sets a poor example for the team he leads.

- **One of the reasons that many people avoid leadership is because they do not want to assume responsibility.**

  When the team is losing, the leader is responsible. When the team is winning, the players get the credit. We see this happen routinely in the sports arena. It also happens in business and other organizations. In a nutshell, it is the price of leadership. As a leader, I can tell you that I hate when I lose for our team, but I love when they win for the good of the whole organization. When we agree to accept the role of a leader, we must accept responsibility. From that point forward we can delegate authority to others to *'get the job done,'* but we always retain the responsibility for any failures. This fact makes it very important to pick quality team members. Lou Holts noted that, *"You can loose with good players, but you can't win with bad ones."* In leadership you are responsible for the achievement of the mission.

- **Leaders must define reality, cast a clear vision, and chart the course for how the team will proceed.**

  In order to take a team from *'here'* to *'there'*, two things have to happen. First the team must be convinced that *'here'* is not good enough. Secondly, they have to know that *'there'* is better and worth going to.

It is the leader's job to convince the team that the *'vision'* of *'there'* is better than the reality of *'here.'*

This is a vital function that must not be overlooked. While *'here'* might not be satisfactory to the leader, *'there'* might be seen by members of the team as *'too much work.'* Often the inertia of keeping things as they are, even when they are less than perfect, is stronger than the desire to make things better. Once a destination, *(there),* has been decided, the leader must chart the course. It is his/her responsibility to develop a plan to achieve the mission. Often the process of going from *'here'* to *'there'* becomes *sidetracked* and *confused.* At these times it is a requirement that the leader handles the distraction and re-focuses the team on the vision of *'there.'* To achieve any long term vision there will be times that the team is *off course.* This should not be a cause for panic. It is merely a time for adjustment and modification of the process.

- **Leaders constantly evaluated the team's progress.**
  As the team is on the journey of fulfilling the mission, the leader has the responsibility to *create and maintain momentum* toward the goal. In order to make sure that maximum progress is achieved the leader is paying close attention to what is working, what isn't working, and what needs to be changed. When a leader is able to sustain and build momentum, he looks better than he probably is.

When a leader looses momentum he can look worse than he truly is. Creating and maintaining momentum makes leadership more fun and easier.

- **Finally, leaders initiate.**

   Leaders tend to have a bias for action. They are often ready to move and make things happen. It is the leader that usually sees the future first and sees the farthest. He/she is usually the first to step out, and call for action. When leaders lag behind it usually communicates negatively to the followers.

Some Traits of Leaders

- **Leaders are Readers.**

   Leaders are people that are interested in self development. The hardest person I've ever lead is me! In order to lead myself, I have to be constantly learning and becoming a better example for myself. It is very important that I maintain healthy self respect. It is impossible to act differently than the way you see yourself. For the reason I and most leaders understand that we must develop ourselves first.

- **People always ask if leaders are born or made.**

   There are no unborn leaders, but there are people that are born with more natural ability for leadership than others. Of course, there are people born with more musical talent than others. The truth is that leadership can be learned, and if one is born with a leaning toward leadership it is easier to learn.

- **It strikes me that many leaders grow exponentially through crucible experiences.**

  This occurs when we are challenged in a tremendously significant way. Maybe it is an overwhelming *'management'* challenge, health issues, family problems, or a million other things. It is an experience that changes our world view in a way that drastically affects our view of, and ability for, leadership. As we grow in leadership, we are continuously accepting more and more responsibility. Accepting new challenges, working with different types of people, and leading in different cultural settings, can add to our leadership growth. Crucible experiences however, are those that really become a *'watershed'* of growth, and it is easy to see a major difference in our outcomes before and after these experiences. In some cases it manifests itself in our taking on a completely new leadership role.

I mentioned above that **'Leaders are Readers'** and that simple fact is not only true but necessary to maintain and to increase your leadership skills. I have often referred to John Maxwell and the gems of leadership that he has shared with the world.

I have read many of John Maxwell's books and have tucked little *'Leadership Gems'* away for my future coaching or training of **Leadership Skills**.

Two very strong points I gained from John Maxwell's book, *"The 21 Irrefutable Laws of Leadership,"* that helps to drive home the need for Leaders to continue honing their skills through reading are; **The Law of the Picture** and **The Law of the Big Mo.**

- *The Law of the Picture.*
  "People Do What People See," is a great example of a powerful part of leadership. It is vital that the leader always set a positive example for those he/she seeks to lead.

- *The Law of the Big Mo.*
  When you have momentum nothing hurts, and when you lose momentum, everything hurts.

Also, in John Maxwell's book *"Attitude 101"* he explains the importance of *'Maintaining a Positive Attitude'* as a must for anyone who seeks to lead others.

Attitude sets the tone, not only for the leader but for the individuals following him.

Attitude...

It is the advance man of our true selves

Its roots are inward, but its fruits are outward

It is our best friend or our worse enemy

It is more honest & more consistent than our words

It is an outward look based on past experiences

It is a thing which draws or propels people to them

It is never content until it is expressed

It is the librarian of our past.

It is the speaker of our present

It is the prophet of our future

Questions for Review

1. Do I have a better understanding of what is needed in a Business Plan?

2. Do I understand the value of a Professional Support Team?

3. Have I gained a better understanding of the Accounting needs of a small business?

4. Do I now have a better understanding of Financial Statements?

5. Will I be able to develop Management Footprints and understand some key Business Ratios?

6. Do I understand the need to develop Internal Control sensors?

7. Did the Legal chapter give me a better understanding of an attorney's value to my company?

8. Do I now understand the informational needs of the banker?

9. Did the chapter on Insurance give me a better understanding of a company's insurance needs?

10. Did the Government chapter inspire me to become more aware of government functions and responsibilities?

11. Was I surprised at the expansion of regulations relative to small businesses?

12. Did the Leadership chapter give me a heads up toward the development of leadership in my business?

Hopefully your answers to the above twelve questions were **"Yes."** Don't worry; this was not a graded test, just questions to help you get the most out of this book. The important thing is; you now own a "Beginner's Guide Book" that can be used as a reference book as long as you need it in the future. Put it to good use, re-read the chapters you didn't fully understand; than develop your company into one structured to obtain the direction needed for a profitable and manageable operation.

About the Author
RG Bud Phelps

RG Bud Phelps was born in Gibbon, Nebraska, in 1932. He lived there until his family moved to Curtis, Nebraska starting in 1944, and continuing until 1951 when he enlisted in the U.S. Navy.

He graduated from the Nebraska School of Agriculture (NSA) in 1949, which was the only agriculture high school in the state.

He attended Kearney State Teachers College (now the University of Nebraska at Kearney) 1950-51, and again in 1955-56.

He served in the U.S. Navy from 1951 to 1955, being stationed at two Naval Air Stations (Quonset Point, RI and Atlantic City, NJ), and with the VC-4 Squadron aboard the USS Valley Forge CVS-45.

He graduated from the University of Denver in 1958, with a BSBA degree/emphasis in Accounting.

While attending the University of Denver he worked for a public accounting firm (Price Waterhouse).

From that point forward he worked in private accounting positions gaining valuable accounting experiences over 50 years, working first for Jolly Rancher Candy Company in Colorado and last for his own pet products manufacturing and marketing company in Grand Island, Nebraska.

He married, Patricia Kelly, in 1955, and they are currently living in Lincoln, Nebraska. Bud and Pat enjoy spending time with family; including their three daughters, son-in-laws, four grandkids and one great grandson; all which presently live in Lincoln.

Bud's Business books

"Cover Your Nut" – *Practical Accounting in Plain English for the Real World.*

"The Business Plan & *Beyond"* – *Beginners Guide Book*

Bud's Historical Fiction books

"Gibbon's Secrets" – *A Boy's Memories of the 40's*

"Back in the Day" – *1945-1955 (High School, summers between, and U.S. Navy*

In the works – Fiction Mystery – *"Mills Park Mystery"*